My Arctic Adventure

# By Truck to the North

## By Andy Turnbull
## with Debora Pearson

Annick Press • Toronto • New York • Vancouver

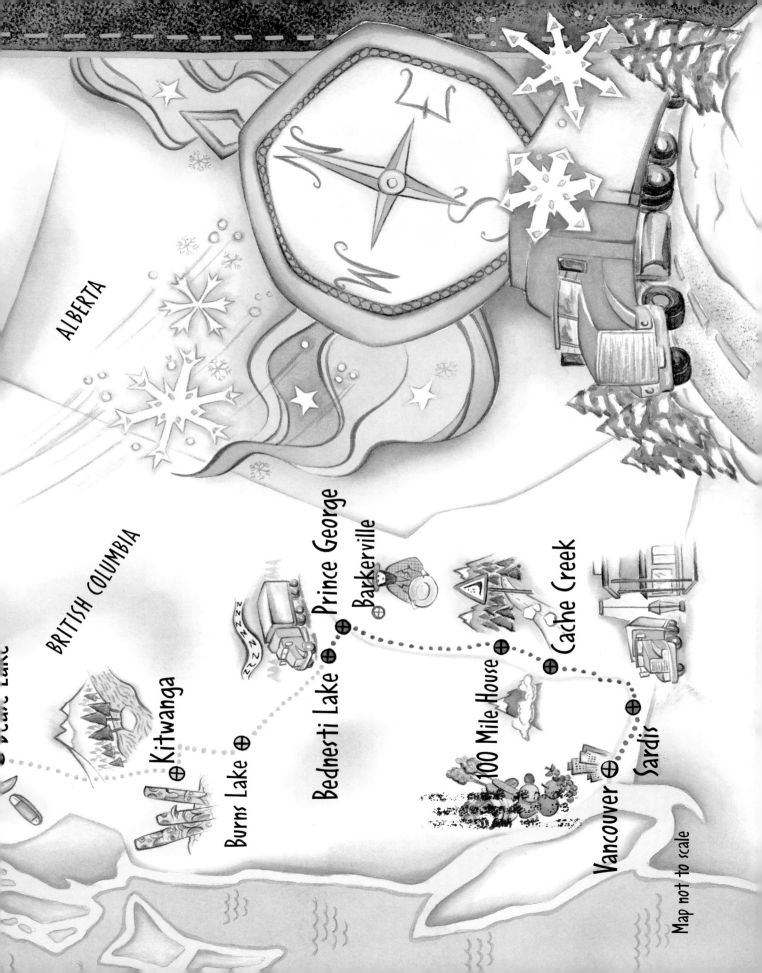

ALBERTA

BRITISH COLUMBIA

Kitwanga

Burns Lake

Bednesti Lake

Prince George

Barkerville

100 Mile House

Cache Creek

Vancouver

Sardis

Map not to scale

# Moose on the Loose!

**W**e were driving down an icy hill when Bill spotted the tracks heading out of the bush and toward the narrow road. By the time I saw them, just beyond the truck's headlight beams, Bill had already reacted. He stepped on the brake pedal, peered through the dark for the owner of the tracks — and that's when we saw the young bull moose on the road below us. We were headed straight for him!

Bill slammed on the brakes, but it didn't make much difference. Even good brakes can't hold an 18-wheeler back for long on a steep, slippery hill. We couldn't swing around the moose: the road was too narrow and our truck was too big. All we could do was hold on tight and hope the moose would get out of our way. He didn't have a moment to spare.

The moose broke into a panicky run away from us. As he turned to the side of the road, he slipped and fell. I thought he was a goner, but at the last moment he scrambled to his feet, jumped out of our path and into the darkness. He was safe. It was the last we saw of him before we sped past.

"Now that was close," Bill breathed out the words. "Too close. If we had hit him, that would have been it for the moose and probably the front of this truck, too. That's how my first truck got wrecked."

**The moose started to run …**

# By Truck to the North

**M**oose on the road are just one of the problems that Bill Rutherford has to worry about. He's a long-distance trucker. But driving an 18-wheel tractor trailer is only part of his work.

Bill also buys goods in one place and sells them in another. To me, Bill is a kind of merchant adventurer, like Marco Polo. Marco Polo, many people believe, travelled all the way from Europe to China and back over 700 years ago. The goods that Marco Polo and other ancient merchants brought back to Europe – including silk, spices, and gunpowder – were already well-known in the Far East. But those same goods were unfamiliar to people in the west. The fruits and vegetables that Bill carries in his truck are like that too. Most of them are common in the south. But in the far north, where fruit trees and vegetable crops can't grow, or aren't grown, even ordinary things like fresh lettuce, apples, and potatoes seem like exotic treats.

Bill travels along a totally different route than Marco Polo did – he starts out in Vancouver, British Columbia, where he buys fruits and vegetables and groceries. He carries his goods with him to Inuvik, a town north of the Arctic Circle, and beyond. Inuvik is so far north that there's no sun for an entire month during the winter. That's because this part of the globe is tilted away from the sun in the wintertime. During the summer, it's the opposite: the sun is up for 24 hours a day for almost two whole months.

North of Inuvik is the community of Tuktoyaktuk. During winter, when the waters of the Mackenzie

Bill and his truck go everywhere together. To reach the Arctic, they head over huge mountains, into frozen forests, and along routes used by gold rush miners over a hundred years ago.

River freeze solid enough to support a big truck, Bill drives up the river and out on the Beaufort Sea to reach "Tuk." The roads Bill travels on for this part of his journey are called ice roads because that's what they're made of – not pavement or gravel or dirt like regular roads, just frozen water. Ice roads are the only land routes open during winter in parts of the Arctic. But these roads can be deadly if the ice breaks up while a truck is on it.

When it comes to danger and surprises, Bill has faced almost everything, from blizzards in July to winds that are powerful enough to blow a truck right off the road. Bill's round trip covers about 5,000 miles (8,045 kilometres) – more than one-fifth the distance you must travel to circle the world at its widest point. There's no doubt about it: that's some truck trip!

I've spent much of my life travelling with truckers all over the world and writing about my adventures with them. Travelling by truck has allowed me to see remote, distant places that I wouldn't have been able to reach otherwise. Along the way, I have met lots of people and made some new friends. When I travel by truck, I feel like I'm part of another world, a world where people are easy to get to know and the next adventure is just up the road.

Riding with Bill gave me a chance to do two things I had always wanted to do: see the Arctic by truck and drive over its strange, dangerous ice roads. As I soon found out, travelling with Bill was the adventure I hoped it would be – and much more!

What's made of frozen water and is strong enough for trucks to drive on? An Arctic ice road! When this one melts away in the spring, all that will be left is a wide, deep river.

Vancouver ⊕

By the time we finished buying everything on Bill's huge grocery list, we had enough food to last 500 people for an entire month.

We picked up some huge bags of dog food here. Although I couldn't say for sure, I think TD liked this stop!

The apples in Bill's truck had come from an orchard east of Vancouver, in the Okanagan Valley.

# Chapter 1

# Tail Wagging Fun

**Doggone it, there's nothing like the view from inside Bill's cab.**

"All set, TD?" asked Bill. TD wagged her tail eagerly and stood up in Bill's lap, resting her front paws on the steering wheel. Seeing TD like that made me laugh — she looked like she could hardly wait for us to get on our way.

TD's full name is "The Dog" and she keeps Bill company on all his trips. When I first saw her, I was surprised to find out that she was going with us. Where would TD stay? Wouldn't she be cooped up in the truck all day? Dogs, even small ones like TD, didn't go on long-distance truck trips … or did they?

I soon learned that TD was the perfect companion to have on our trip. When she wanted to see out the windows, she stood up in Bill's lap, just like she was doing

# A Juicy Adventure

KAWAKAMI ORCHARDS

The apples in Bill's truck had been on a journey, even before we picked them up. They had begun life in an orchard like this one, east of Vancouver. After the fall harvest, they had been taken to packinghouses, where they were graded and packed into boxes. From there, the apples would go on their greatest adventure — all the way with us to Inuvik and Tuktoyaktuk in the Arctic.

**First, you grab the steering wheel … TD gives me a quick lesson in how to drive Bill's big rig.**

now. Most of the time though, she preferred to sleep on a spot on the floor in front of my seat. When I touched the spot with my hand, I found out why.

"The exhaust pipe passes right under there," explained Bill. "That's why it's nice and warm. If I were a small dog, I would probably sleep there too."

TD hopped from Bill's lap into mine and nestled there. "Better get used to it," grinned Bill, "I think you've just become TD's new favourite place to snooze."

Like TD, I was eager to start our trip. We had already spent an entire day shopping at food warehouses for everything on Bill's gigantic grocery list, then loading his

purchases into the trailer. Bill chooses everything himself, especially the fruits and vegetables. He knows that the fresher his goods are, the better his business will be when it's time to sell them.

By the time we had finished shopping, the huge trailer was three-quarters full. We had it all, everything from coffee and canned soup to tangerines and turnips – enough groceries and produce to last 500 people for an entire month!

Finally we were off. As we drove over a bridge, on our way out of Vancouver, TD and I gazed down at a log boom in the Fraser River. Like us, those logs were taking a trip, too. They had started out in a

**13**

I saw lots of logs as we drove north. Some were on huge logging trucks heading south from the forests. Others, like these logs, were travelling by water to a mill.

forest somewhere up the coast and, after being cut down, had been floated along the water to where we were looking at them. From here, they would travel to a mill where they would be turned into newsprint, cardboard, toilet paper and other wood and paper products, like the boxes in Bill's truck.

I looked away from the logs and thought more about our journey. It was the middle of January, the time of year when the ice on the Mackenzie River is usually thick enough to drive on. What would it be like to drive on an ice road? What adventures would we have before we got there?

"There's no telling what we'll run into," said Bill, as if he had been reading my thoughts. "I'll never forget the time I was driving up the Rat Pass, near the Arctic

**The view: Bill's big truck. Our job: to fill it up!**

14

**T**here's only one thing I like more than looking at a truck — and that's riding in one. Climbing into a truck's cab (the place where the driver and passenger sit) is fun, too. The first thing you need to do before climbing in is grab the door handle and open the door. Handles are often located near the bottom of a truck's doors so you can reach them from the ground. After you've opened the door, you can take the steps up to the cab. Steps are usually on or next to the round tanks found under the doors and under the sleeper (the large "box" at the back of the cab). By the way, those tanks aren't just for show — they hold the truck's fuel.

Circle. The winds can get pretty vicious there and on this particular trip I saw a rock that was as big as a baseball. It was being blown by the wind.

"A wind that's strong enough to blow rocks around is one thing. But this wind was something else. It was so powerful that it was blowing the rock uphill, not downhill. If I hadn't seen that sight for myself, I would have hardly believed it.

"Who knows what the three of us will see this time as we head to Tuktoyaktuk?"

**That's Bill fueling up at the pumps.**

Fuel islands are a busy part of a truck stop because trucks go through a lot of fuel. An almost empty truck takes more than ten times the amount of fuel needed to fill a car.

# Chapter 2

# A Truck Stop Story

**W**hile Bill fueled up at the truck stop, I let TD out of the cab and played with her, away from the other trucks and cars. If you keep a dog in a truck you have to play with it every day so that it gets enough exercise. TD got a real workout with me because I had a rubber ball that I threw across the parking lot and against a brick wall. TD never quite caught the ball before it reached the bricks. When it bounced off the wall, she had to chase the ball almost all the way back to me before she could finally grab it in her mouth!

# Where Am I Now?

Bill didn't buy much fuel here because they were selling "summer fuel." For our trip, we needed cold-weather "winter fuel." In the far north, we might buy "Arctic fuel."

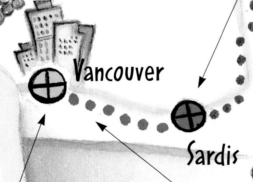

Vancouver

Sardis

Before we began our journey, Bill inspected his truck to make sure everything was working properly. I helped him check the brake lights.

We stopped at a weigh scale here. Trucks are weighed to make sure they're loaded properly and aren't carrying more weight than they should.

**Where can you find women truckers? In the same places you'll spot men who drive trucks: at truck stops and on the road in their rigs. Carol Ann Schlussler (left) and her sister Patricia Rauschnot (right) are both long-distance truckers who drive their own trucks. Like Bill, they each have a dog that sometimes goes on the road with them. That's Tia with Carol Ann and Trixie in Patricia's arms.**

When Bill was finished, we put TD back in the cab where she would be safe and comfortable. Then we went into the 24-hour restaurant for a meal. When most people think of a truck stop, they think of a place that serves up fuel and food to truckers and car drivers on the road. But there's more to a truck stop than that.

A truck stop is like a home away from home for long-distance truckers. It's where they go to catch up on the latest news and gossip, get cleaned up, or just hang out and watch TV in a special truckers' lounge that some truck stops have. A really big truck stop has almost everything that you would find in a small town: a dentist, barbershop, movie theatre, laundromat, church, and some offices and stores.

This truck stop didn't have many fancy features, but Bill and I didn't care. We had done a lot of lifting and loading and what we really wanted was a shower, something

Here's one truck passenger I wouldn't expect to see at a truck stop — a teddy bear named Coco. Coco comes from a school in Wisconsin and goes on the road with truckers. Each driver who gives Coco a ride also sends a postcard back to the kids at Coco's school. I wonder if Coco likes riding with truckers as much as I do …

you couldn't get in our truck and something you could get here. It was time to head over to the other side of the building and get washed up, truck stop style.

We paid a clerk who gave us some soap, towels, and numbered keys to two private washrooms. Each washroom had its own toilet, sink, shower, and bench.

"I'll meet you by the bulletin board when you're through," Bill called over as he unlocked his washroom. "It's by the store."

A truck stop's bulletin board is one of the ways truckers exchange information and stay in touch with each other. It's the place where truckers post notices about trucks and other equipment they want to buy or sell. The bulletin board is also where drivers can advertise that they're looking for work and people with jobs to offer can advertise their openings.

Bill joined me at the board and we walked over to the trucker's store where we bought some antifreeze for the truck. Then it was time to pull out.

"We've got three days of hard driving ahead," said Bill as he climbed back into the cab. "And it could be tough going. Another trucker just warned me about the snow north of the Arctic Circle. He said that it's chest high if you go off the road and end up in a ditch — and when there are whiteouts, it's easy for that to happen."

# Kids and Truckers Get Together

**E**ven with pets for company and other truckers to talk to at truck stops, it's easy for truckers to get lonely while out on the road. That's why some truck drivers belong to Trucker Buddy International Inc., a non-profit program that links together truckers in North America with more than 125,000 kids around the world. Each truck driver in the Trucker Buddy program is assigned to a classroom teacher. The trucker is responsible for sending a postcard, note, or letter to the teacher's students once a week so that the kids can track the driver's travels. In return, the class writes to the truck driver at least once a month. Many Trucker Buddy kids, including the ones shown above, also get the chance to meet their trucker pen pals face to face and inspect big rigs up close!

For more on the Trucker Buddy program, visit its website at: http://www.layover.com/truckerbuddy.htm

# Truck Stop Stuff

 Truckers often spend the night parked at a truck stop. Some truck stops have parking lots that can hold more than 700 trucks at one time.

What's on the menu at many truck stop restaurants? Bacon 'n' eggs and burgers, french toast and fruit pies, salads and quiche, and more!

From phones at the restaurant tables to places to plug in computers, some truck stops have everything drivers need to stay in touch with others.

 A really big truck stop has almost everything you would find in a small town, including a beauty parlour, post office, shopping mall, and offices.

Some truck stops don't have any locks on their doors. Why? Because they are always open: 24 hours a day, every single day of the year.

I looked down at the Fraser River
and thought about the people
who had come here one hundred
and fifty years ago in search of
gold. They had seen a similar
view but without the road

# Chapter 3

# Thrills, Chills, and Hills

As we drove up the mountain, I rolled down my window and reached out to touch the cloud. It hung near the top of the mountain and, from a distance, it looked soft and puffy, like you could hang on to it. But up close, the cloud was almost invisible. When I tried to grab it, my hand passed through mist and fog. There was nothing for me to hold onto — unless you counted some tiny drops of cold water!

Clouds were all around us as we followed the TransCanada Highway to the town of Cache Creek, at the top of the Fraser Canyon. We drove up and down many hills, climbing high into the clouds and dipping into the valleys, again and again. Every so often, I glimpsed the Fraser River and some towns below me in the bottom of the canyon. Everything looked distant and unreal.

This was the area where gold had been found, beginning a century and a half ago, during an exciting time known as the Fraser River Gold Rush. Further up the road, near Barkerville, we would enter the region where the Cariboo Gold Rush (named after the nearby Cariboo Mountains) took place over a hundred years ago, after the Fraser gold finds.

# Where Am I Now?

**Bednesti Lake**

**Prince George**

**Barkerville**

During the gold rush, bankers, miners, and merchants lived here. Later, after the gold rush ended, Barkerville became a ghost town. Today, it's a "living museum" with restored buildings.

From inside my warm sleeping bag in the cab, I listened to wolves howling off in the distance.

**100 Mile House**

Back in the days of stagecoach travel, this had been a place where horses and passengers took a much-needed break during their journeys.

Danger ahead! Rocks the size of a washing machine had fallen near here.

**Cache Creek**

**Sardis**

What did a soft, puffy cloud feel like? High in the mountains, I touched one and found out.

# Old-Fashioned Horsepower

**A century ago, there was no paved road running through the Cariboo region. If Bill had been a merchant heading north in those days, he would have taken the wagon trail these travellers were on and used horses or perhaps camels for getting around.**

It hadn't been easy for the gold seekers to reach the remote areas where gold had been found. They had to follow narrow routes that ran through treacherous waters, in and out of dense forests, and along the edges of towering mountains. Mules, ponies – even camels purchased from the U.S. Army – were used to carry the miners' supplies through here. If Bill had been a travelling merchant during gold rush times, he might have used camels to carry his goods in this area. Now that would have been some sight!

Bill swung the truck around a big rock in the road and pointed to the highway crew nearby. They were using a loader to pick up boulders that had tumbled down the mountain. Some of the rocks were the size of a washing machine.

Bill shook his head. "If one of those ever hit a car, it would smash it flat."

I got my head out of the clouds and took a second look around. We were in a dangerous place. Road signs warned of falling rocks and part of the mountain was actually wrapped in a net made of chain-

What was it like to be part of the gold rush? To find out, visit Barkerville. Once a booming town during gold rush days, Barkerville today is a "living museum" that has restored buildings and staff in period costumes. You can ride a stagecoach down the streets, pan for gold (see above) or talk about the good old days with others by the wheel once used to power the local grain mill (see left).

**While Bill checked the engine, I thought about the danger of frostbite — it was very cold out.**

link fence to keep it from crumbling onto the road. It seemed that it was just a matter of time before the entire mountain fell apart. When that happened, a giant rock slide would probably bury the road and anything else – trucks, cars, people – that was on it. It would take a gigantic road crew to deal with a disaster like that.

We continued driving and, after we left Cache Creek, we climbed steadily into the mountains. The air grew colder and colder. Back in Vancouver, it had been warm enough for people to play golf by the bare highway, even though it was wintertime. But here, snow covered the sides of the road and a pile of it lay between the lanes. I glanced down at TD snoozing by the exhaust pipe. It was a

good night to be inside Bill's heated cab.

Most truckers, including Bill, usually spend the night parked at a truck stop, if there's one nearby. We weren't close to one, so we found the next best thing: a restaurant parking lot in Bednesti Lake, north of Prince George. Then it was time for all of us to get ready for bed.

Some trucks have two bunks in the sleeper part of their cabs, but Bill's has only one bunk. Fortunately, it's big enough for two people. When truckers sleep two in a bunk, they usually arrange themselves so that one person's head is next to the other person's feet. That way, if one person snores he won't snore in the other person's ear.

Sleeping in a truck is sort of like sleeping in a cozy cave. There's not much room,

# Inside a Truck's Cab

 A truck's cab is more than the place where a driver and a passenger sit. After a hard day on the road, a cab becomes a living room – the perfect place for relaxing, reading, and taking a break from driving.

 A long-distance trucker's cab has a bedroom at the back. This part of the cab is called the "sleeper." A sleeper is large enough to hold at least one bunk. The bunks are ready to use and never folded away.

 What else will you find in a sleeper? Lights to use while reading in bed, fans that circulate air, and lots of storage space. There are places to store a TV (if the trucker has one), clothing, and extra bedding.

 Some trucks' cabs have little kitchens, complete with coffee makers, microwave ovens and refrigerators. Cabs can also have toilets and showers that use a water supply carried by the truck.

 Some things sound different inside a cab. Take the ordinary sound of rain: there's nothing like hearing it plonking away on the roof of the cab while you're warm and dry inside.

Here's one view of the front of a cab, taken from the bunk at the back. Coffee, anyone?

Sleeping here is like sleeping in a cozy cave. There's not much room, but it's comfortable.

30

This cab has two bunks.

From this bunk, you can watch TV, use the computer, or pick out some clothes to wear.

Camels in B.C. Introdu
in May, 1862 by Frank Lau

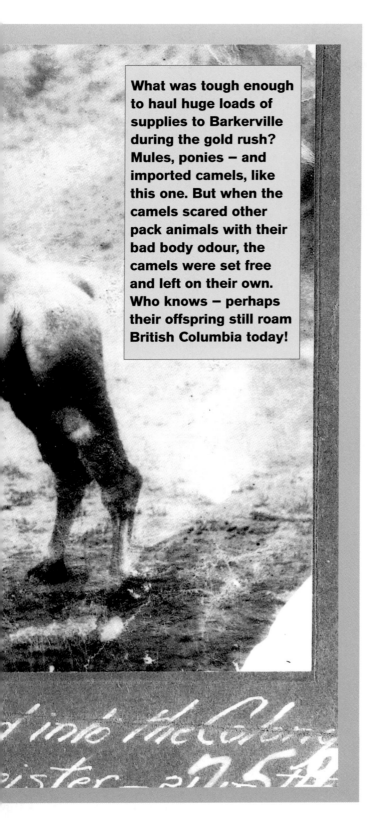

What was tough enough to haul huge loads of supplies to Barkerville during the gold rush? Mules, ponies – and imported camels, like this one. But when the camels scared other pack animals with their bad body odour, the camels were set free and left on their own. Who knows – perhaps their offspring still roam British Columbia today!

**Like any bed, Bill's bunk can be used as a seat.**

but I like it. The bunk is comfortable, there are places above and below it to store your stuff, and, in Bill's sleeper, there's even a spot for TD's bed. As I got in the bunk, I watched her hop into a soft, padded box on the floor of the sleeper. Then she curled up, and closed her eyes.

We drew the curtain between the sleeper and the rest of the cab, then shut off the lights. From inside my warm sleeping bag, I heard wolves calling to each other off in the distance.

After a while, their howls faded away. I wondered where the wolves were going and what they would find along the way.

I liked kicking up the fresh snow
under my feet. TD had other ideas.
She liked running and sliding in it.

## Chapter 4

# Winter Wonderland

Plop! TD skidded through the snow and landed on her face. When she stood up, she wagged her tail and gave me a dog-style grin as if to say, "This white stuff is fun to play in, but it sure is cold and slippery!"

The parking lot had been dusted with a fresh layer of snow overnight and that seemed to please Bill too, but only for a moment. "The snow makes for nice driving because the road is smoother," he said. "But it also means there's more danger of moose on the highway. It's easier for them to walk there than go through deep snow in the bush. And at this time of year, moose like to lick the salt they find on the road, too."

We put some food in the truck for TD, then headed to the restaurant to get some breakfast for ourselves. We were part of the way through our meal when another trucker came in and asked if there was a repair shop around. There was something wrong with his truck but he couldn't tell what it was.

"The closest place is about half an

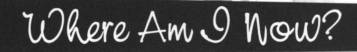

Moose on the loose! This was where we had a close call I'll never forget.

The jade that comes from the mines here is used to make jewellery, carvings – and the handles of the pocketknives I saw at a truck stop down the road.

⊕ Dease Lake

This island was once part of a nearby mountain. It had fallen in the water during an avalanche.

Kitwanga ⊕

People from all over come to see the totem poles here.

Burns Lake ⊕

Bednesti Lake

Bill lived in this town when he was younger. He showed me the log cabin his grandparents built here decades ago.

36

**The creatures carved in these towering cedar poles have ancient meaning. They represent the history and traditions of the native people who lived in Kitwanga.**

hour away," replied Bill. "Let me take a look – maybe I can give you a hand."

I finished eating my eggs while Bill and the other trucker walked over to a truck with its hood open. A few minutes later Bill returned alone and sat back down.

"It's just an air leak, nothing serious," he grinned. "That guy's from the south and he thinks this is cold. I told him that you and I were going all the way to the Arctic. When I mentioned the ice roads we'd have to take to reach Tuktoyaktuk, he just shook his head. I don't think he believed me – he muttered something about how a truck couldn't possibly drive on a layer of ice without crashing through it!"

We paid for our meals, joined TD back in the cab, and turned onto the highway once more. North of the ancient native fort of Kitwanga, I spotted an island in the fast-

# Jade: The Inside Story

Jade miners use giant diamond saws, like the one above, to cut into boulders containing jade, which is harder than steel. The dark green jade found in the boulder at the bottom will be used to make jewellery and carvings.

# What Did You Say?

**W**hen some truckers talk on their CB ("citizen band") radios, they use colourful, often humorous expressions instead of ordinary words and phrases. Can you match the CB slang on the left with its correct meaning on the right? The answers are below.

| | | | |
|---|---|---|---|
| 1. | boardwalk | a. | large piece of tire on the road |
| 2. | roller skate | b. | truck stop restaurant |
| 3. | thermos bottle | c. | trucker's return trip |
| 4. | window wash | d. | bumpy road |
| 5. | eat-em-up | e. | truck weigh station |
| 6. | dragon wagon | f. | road construction |
| 7. | flip flop | g. | tanker truck |
| 8. | destruction | h. | small car |
| 9. | alligator | i. | rainstorm |
| 10. | chicken coop | j. | tow truck |

**Answers: 1d, 2h, 3g, 4i, 5b, 6j, 7c, 8f, 9a, 10e**

flowing river that ran near the road. The island was the size of a house and dotted with trees. I was surprised to see it there: I thought that the water would have washed an island away a long time ago.

"That's a new island," Bill told me when I asked him about it. He pointed to some wide scars in the mountains by the river. "See those marks? A couple of winters back, an avalanche of snow tore a chunk out of that hill and dumped it in the river. Those trees you see on the island are the same ones that were growing in it when it used to be part of the mountain!"

I looked at the foot of the mountain, where the scars ended. Piles of broken trees lay scattered as if a giant had flung

them around. Like the falling rocks we had seen on the highway the day before, an avalanche could cause a lot of damage.

After it grew dark, we pulled into a truck stop for some supper. But this wasn't just a spot to grab a quick meal on the road – it was also a place where I learned something new, something I found surprising.

As I walked past the cash register, I spotted some interesting-looking pocket-knives for sale. They had green handles made of jade. Jade is a mineral used to make beautiful, sometimes costly objects and the only jade I knew of came from China and other far-off places. But not this jade – the man behind the counter told me that it had come from a mine north of the

If you get too close to the swirling snow that's thrown and blown around by this truck, you could find yourself in the middle of a whiteout!

**Moose are the biggest members of the deer family. Moose "cousins" include white-tailed deer and caribou.**

**Baby moose are tough. By the time a moose is a few days old, it can swim well and run about as fast as you can.**

**Male moose are called "bulls." They usually grow and shed a set of antlers each year. Some full-grown bulls have antlers that measure more than 1.5 metres (5 feet) between the widest points.**

**A large adult moose has a huge appetite. If you added up all the twigs, leaves, and plants a moose eats in a single day, its food would weigh about as much as a four-year-old child.**

**It usually takes a pack of wolves to bring down a single moose. It's not easy for wolves to hunt and kill moose — the wolves are successful only once out of every 12 times that they attempt a moose attack.**

**Bawling, bellowing, roaring — a moose can make a mighty sound, especially during mating season!**

truck stop, near Dease Lake. I was looking at jade from British Columbia, local jade! I gazed at the pocketknives for a long time — they reminded me that unexpected and strange things were all around me. What else would I discover?

I soon had an answer to my question. After we got back on the road and drove down an icy hill, we had our close call with the young moose. It happened just as Bill had said it might happen — the moose wandered out on the road because it was easier for it to walk there than in the bush. As Bill called other truckers on his CB radio to warn them about the moose on the loose, I peered through the windshield for other dangers. All I could see were falling crystals of snow that sparkled like tiny diamonds in the truck's headlights.

We were the only ones on the highway until a southbound truck roared past us, swirling snow everywhere. We plunged into a whiteout — and the road vanished.

Make way for moose!
On roads, across snow,
moose really go places.

During the Klondike Gold Rush, so many Americans poured into the Canadian city of Dawson that American flags were flown here and Fourth of July celebrations were held.

2337. FRONT STREET DAWSON JULY 4th 99

# A Blast into the Past

The snow whirled around us, covering everything in sight. Then, as suddenly as it had begun, the whiteout cleared. Tiny diamonds of snow reappeared. The other truck was gone and soon its tracks disappeared, wiped away by the wind. We were alone.

As the snow drifted down, I thought about other adventurers who had passed through this part of the north. About a hundred years ago, people in search of Klondike gold had travelled from Skagway in Alaska, west of us, over the steep and icy Chilkoot Pass. Once they and their supplies made it over the Pass – *if* they made it – those people journeyed by boat and raft along the Klondike River system to Dawson City and the gold fields near it. Back then, there was no road to follow, like the one we would take tomorrow to reach

# Where Am I Now?

**DEMPSTER HIGHWAY**

Dempster Highway

Unlike most other highways, this one is a gravel road that covers permafrost.

## Dawson City ✛

TD and I looked out on a pale, frozen forest ...

During the winter of 1910–11, members of the Mounties' "Lost Patrol" died of cold and starvation on their way to Dawson City.

Klondike Highway

**CINNAMON BUN**

### Braeburn Lodge ✛

## Whitehorse ✛

This stop made my mouth water. Huge, sugary cinnamon buns are baked and sold here. Even the local airstrip is named after them!

Alaska Highway

### Skagway ✛

A century ago, gold seekers arrived here, then crossed a steep pass on foot. Those who made it to the other side rafted along the Klondike River to the gold fields.

## Watson Lake ✛

It felt like we were in the middle of nowhere, but Bill found a parking lot where we spent the night.

**In this frozen forest, even ordinary trees looked unfamiliar when coated with ice crystals.**

Dawson, and no modern conveniences and comforts along the route, like the truck stops we had visited further south.

But the gold prospectors' journey and our journey did have some things in common: both were difficult, lonely trips through a part of the world most people didn't know about. Some things hadn't changed very much in a hundred years.

I looked over at the clock on the dashboard. It was almost midnight. I wondered where we would spend the night. Last night, we had slept in a parking lot. But there couldn't be any restaurants or other places with parking lots out here …

Just north of the border between British Columbia and the Yukon Territories,

Bill surprised me by pulling off the road. I couldn't believe my eyes – we were turning into an empty parking lot next to a store and set of gas pumps! It was just the place to get a good night's sleep.

The next day, as we headed toward Dawson City, we drove down into a valley. There, TD and I looked out on a pale, frozen forest: the trees nearest the road were covered in hoarfrost. Bill told me that the hoarfrost was caused by exhaust from passing cars and trucks. Exhaust is made partly of tiny water drops that usually disappear in the air. But in this valley, where the temperatures were bone-chilling and the air was extremely still, the water droplets hung around the trees and froze

**This lone moose doesn't know it, but he's on a highway called the Dempster Highway. The gravel covers permanently frozen ground.**

into a thick coating of crystals. It was so cold here that I could feel a chill inside the cab, even with the heater running.

We drove for hours along the floor of the valley without seeing any lights but our own. Finally we spotted some up ahead. They grew bigger and brighter until one car, then another, passed us heading south. "Rush hour," smiled Bill.

After Dawson, we headed onto the Dempster Highway and entered the area where the Lost Patrol had made its long treks. Suddenly, a buzzer sounded on the dashboard. The truck's air pressure had dropped dangerously low. If it fell any more, our brakes wouldn't work. "The compressor is frozen," said Bill. "The same thing happened here on my last trip."

He pulled over by the side of the highway, then suited up. It was time to step out into the cold. He had to open the hood,

In some places around Dawson, you can still find the old wooden cabins built and used by miners during the Klondike Gold Rush (above). When the miners weren't sleeping or eating in their cabins, they were hard at work, like the miner on the left. Next to him is a rocker box, used to separate gold from the worthless dirt and water.

**Bill's truck with its hood open plus a lonely, wintry road equals trouble on the Dempster.**

disconnect the air lines, and pour anti-freeze in them to thaw the compressor.

Bill opened his door and a blast of icy air shoved me over to the other side of the truck. "Better make sure you are well-covered if you're thinking of joining me outside," Bill warned. "It's easy to get frostbite when it's this cold. All you need is some exposed skin and you could end up with some serious pain or worse."

I nodded. I knew that frostbite was an injury caused by severe cold. Frostbite could cause so much permanent damage that the injured area – anything from an ear to a leg – would have to be amputated. I had also heard that, under rare conditions, it was possible for a person to get frostbite on their eyes – and I didn't want to find out what *that* would be like!

Corporal Demp
R. N. W. M. P. – R
Return to Da
Remains Of Th

48

Leader Of The
Patrol After
Having Found
Ft Mac

U ntil its final journey, the "Lost Patrol" was simply one of the patrols organized and led by the Royal Northwest Mounted Police almost a hundred years ago. The patrol's mission was to watch over and protect the people and land of the Canadian north. To do this, four men and a dog team made regular expeditions along a trail from Fort McPherson to Dawson City, a journey of about 800 kilometres (530 miles).

During the winter of 1910-11, the men and their dog team set out from Fort McPherson on a routine patrol. However, as they entered the mountains, they soon became lost in the blowing snow. The men turned back, hoping to reach safety. Exhausted, cold, and starving, they finally died near Fort McPherson. The remains of the "Lost Patrol" were discovered by Corporal Dempster of the Mounted Police (see near left), the Mountie after whom the Dempster Highway is named.

**Watching the northern lights made me feel as tiny and unimportant as one of the snowflakes that I had seen earlier that day. I couldn't stop staring.**

# Chapter 6

# Into an Icy Desert

"It looks like we're in for a show tonight," said Bill, peering up at the strange blurs and streaks of colour beyond our windshield. He stopped the truck by the side of the road and stepped out. Our last stop had been made so that Bill could fix the compressor. That had been a tough, unpleasant job.

But this time, all of us were eager to stop the truck and get out. The midnight lights were glowing – and we didn't want to miss them!

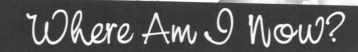

Once we crossed the Arctic Circle, we entered the land of the midnight sun.

Arctic Circle

The conditions were so harsh here that these tiny trees would never grow tall. Perhaps they would live forever ...

I saw a northern lights show here. It was so cold out that I "burned" my hand when I touched the truck door.

This is the place where a trucker named Ken had a funny encounter with some caribou.

**These tiny trees were half my height. Although they looked young, they were really very old.**

The truck's thermometer read -49°C (-56°F) as I zipped up my parka, then looked around for my mittens. They weren't in their usual place, but I stepped outside anyway and shoved my hands deep in the pockets of my parka.

A huge panel of northern lights filled the sky. As soon as I gazed up at it, I couldn't look away. Everything else – me, Bill, the big truck – seemed as small and unimportant as one of the snowflakes that I had seen earlier that day.

I watched until my neck hurt and I felt the cold creeping around my hood. Then, without thinking, I reached for the handle of the truck door with my bare hand. Yeeee-ow!

I yanked my arm back and looked down at my throbbing hand. The freezing metal handle had "burned" it! I later learned that the tiny cells in my skin had frozen and formed ice crystals. It had all happened in an instant – and it really hurt.

My hand was still sore the next morning but I had other, more important things to think about. Today we would cross the Arctic Circle, drive on our first ice road, and finally arrive in the town of Inuvik.

We drove through Ogilvie Valley, then climbed to a plateau, a level area of land in the mountains. This plateau was covered with trees half my height. Although they looked very young, most of the trees were actually quite old. Someone had told me that these miniature trees had grown from seeds that blew up from the valleys. The conditions here are so harsh that the trees would never mature and grow to their full height. I looked at them and wondered if they might live forever …

As we neared Eagle Plains, Bill pointed out some caribou tracks. Seeing the tracks reminded me of a story that a trucker named Ken had told me. I had met Ken on another trucking trip I'd been on.

"This must be around the place where

**You might think this is the place where you actually cross the Arctic Circle – but it's not!**

Ken had a close call with some caribou," I told Bill. "He was coming around a corner when he found about fifty caribou asleep out on the road. Ken hit the brakes and sounded his horn, but the caribou just stood up and looked at him until he had almost stopped. Then they began running ahead of the truck, up the road."

"Ken couldn't build up any speed with the caribou blocking his way so he spun out going up a hill. He had to stop and when he did, the caribou stopped, too, and watched him. Then, when Ken got going again, they started running in front of him, just like they did before. 'Now *that* was irritating!' Ken said."

Every trucker who has crossed Eagle Plains has a tale to tell about the powerful winds that blow here. My favourite one is the story about the driver who was hauling an empty trailer across the plains. When he looked in his mirror, he got a big shock. Two wheels of his trailer were in the air and only the weight of his tractor kept the whole thing from blowing over!

# Land of the Midnight Sun

For people who live in the Arctic, winter days can be long. The sun doesn't rise above the horizon for about a month and there is little sunlight at that time. But in summer, things look much brighter. For two months or so, the sun doesn't set – there is daylight for 24 hours a day and the sun is up at midnight!

The northern lights are colourful. They can be green, pink or violet. Red lights are very rare.

Some of the best places to see the northern lights are in the far northern part of the globe. Two great locations are Yellowknife, in Canada, and Barrow, Alaska. It is often possible to see the lights in some southern locations, as well.

The best time to spot the lights is on a clear, dark night around midnight. The best times of year to see some really dazzling displays are around September 21 and March 21.

Is it possible to hear, as well as see, the northern lights? According to the ancient beliefs of some Inuit people, the lights sometimes swish and make crackling sounds. The Inuit believed that the lights were the souls of the dead who lived in the sky and liked to play games of soccer.

Over the centuries, the spectacular sight of the northern lights has filled some people with terror and others with pleasure and delight. Some people believed that the northern lights foreshadowed disasters and other horrible events. Others believed the lights had healing powers.

**T**he northern lights are caused by giant electrical particle "storms" in the upper atmosphere around Earth.

These dazzling lights appear as rays, bands, or curtains of light. No two displays are ever exactly the same.

We had better luck than that trucker — the winds weren't very strong and we made it across the plains without any trouble. I knew we were close to the Arctic Circle and I could hardly wait to see the sign that marked the place we would cross it.

It would be impossible to notice the Arctic Circle if there wasn't a sign telling you exactly where it is. The Arctic Circle is an invisible line of latitude that marks the location across the north where the sun doesn't rise for one day each winter *and* the sun doesn't set for one day each summer. When you drive north of the Circle, you enter the polar region — and that was something I had always wanted to do!

I enjoyed seeing caribou – but only when they were away from the road and our truck!

**In the icy Arctic desert I saw mountains, too.**

There was a curve in the road where we actually crossed the Circle, but cars and trucks can't stop there because they could cause an accident. The official sign marking the Arctic Circle is further up the road, where it's safe to pull over and walk around. When we got to the sign, Bill stopped the truck and we all jumped out to take a look. TD was first out of the cab: she ran through the snow, barking and checking out the smells.

I was eager to join TD, but this time I made sure I had my mittens on before I left the truck. Apart from the Antarctic, the Arctic is the coldest place on Earth. It would be easy to get more frostbite here.

When most people think of the Arctic, they think of its extremely cold climate. They also think of it as an area that gets lots of snow, but that part isn't true. The Arctic is so dry that some people describe it as a desert. That's right: a cold desert!

"We're getting close to Inuvik and your first ice road crossing," grinned Bill, as we climbed back in the cab.

I couldn't help grinning, too. What adventures lay ahead in the icy desert?

Many dogsled trips are fun-filled adventures.

# Hot on the Trail of Dogsleds

**W**hen some people think of the far north, they think of snow, freezing temperatures, and dog team travel. In the past, dog-powered sleds were a common form of transportation in some parts of the Arctic. Some native peoples depended on dog teams during hunting trips and other long-distance journeys. And for decades, dogsleds were used by the Royal Canadian Mounted Police (formerly known as the Royal Northwest Mounted Police) during their patrols of northern Canada (see left and page 49).

Today, snowmobiles have replaced dogsleds as a popular, convenient way to get around the Arctic. But you can still find dog teams in the far north today. Dogsled races are held during many northern festivals and celebrations. As well, dog team travel is an attraction offered to tourists (see top left) who are looking for something that gives them a run for their money!

I had heard the howl of a wolf, spotted its tracks in the snow, but had never seen one face to face. Then, in an instant, that changed …

# Wild Times Just Ahead

I held my breath as a timber wolf suddenly appeared on the road. It looked bigger than the wolves I had read and heard about and it was the most graceful creature I'd ever seen. It ran ahead of us, its tail floating behind it. Then it slipped into the bushes and was gone.

I was lucky: few people ever get the chance I'd just had to see a timber wolf in the wild. My luck was about to get even better. The frozen Peel River lay before us — it was time to drive on the first ice road of our trip.

We drove down the river bank, past the ferry that was

# Where Am I Now?

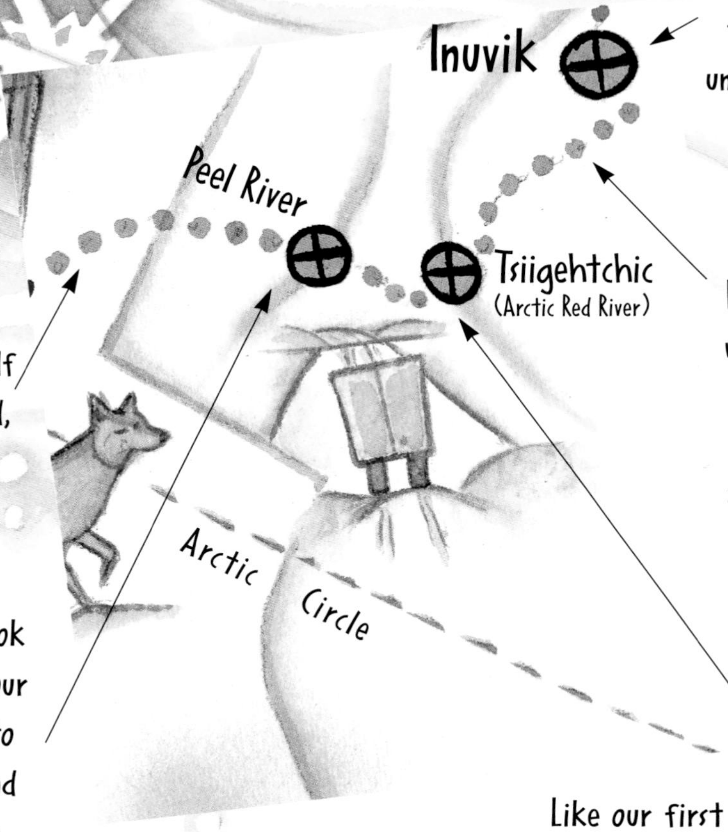

From the utilidors to the Igloo Church, this town was filled with unusual things I couldn't find anywhere else.

**Inuvik** ⊕

**Peel River**

**Tsiigehtchic**
(Arctic Red River) ⊕

By this point, I knew it wouldn't be long before we reached Inuvik. Inuvik was the site of another "first" for me — it was the first Arctic town I had ever visited.

A graceful timber wolf appeared on the road, then disappeared into the bushes.

Arctic Circle

This was where we took the first ice road of our trip. I was surprised to hear the ice crack and pop around us — the sounds were caused by temperature changes, not by our truck driving over the ice.

Like our first ice road crossing, this one was over in minutes — much too soon for me.

# Who's Afraid of the Big Bad Wolf?

**M**any people throughout the centuries have feared and even hated wolves. Why? One reason is that they believed wolves were cold-blooded, cunning hunters that killed humans as well as animals. However, in North America, there have been no known cases of wolves killing people. Unfortunately, there have been many cases of people killing wolves and even wiping them out in some places.

used in the summer and hauled out of the way in the winter. I could tell when the truck's wheels met the frozen river: suddenly, it felt like we were driving on a very bumpy ice rink. And I heard something that made me feel uneasy: the cracking and popping of ice. "That happens when the temperature changes," said Bill. When I glanced at Bill, his face looked almost as serious as mine did. If we hit a frozen-over crack in the ice or broke through the ice, we could be in trouble – big trouble.

Tall snowbanks, made of snow cleared from the road, lay off to the sides. "A thick layer of snow holds in heat," Bill said. "And the heat softens the ice – that's why the snowbanks are over there and we're not."

It took only ten minutes to drive over the Peel, but even on an ice road this short, it was easy to get confused about which way to go. Everything – the white road, the white snowbanks, the white land – looked the same to me. But before I knew it, Bill had brought us safely to the other side of the river and we were climbing up the bank. Our first ice road crossing was over. I was relieved – and disappointed.

But I didn't feel disappointed for very long. About two hours later, we took another ice road, this time over part of the Mackenzie River. Like the Peel River crossing, this crossing was over in minutes –

**In Inuvik, the only place to run sewage and drainage pipes is above ground, in utilidors.**

and this time it seemed too brief to me.

We drove up the river bank toward Inuvik, now only a short distance away. Both Bill and I were anxious to get there. I wanted to see what an Arctic town was like and Bill wanted to meet his customers again and sell lots of goods.

One of the first things I noticed as we drove through town were the utilidors, the fat casings that carry the drainage and sewage pipes to all the buildings in Inuvik. In most towns and cities, drainage and sewage pipes are buried underground where you can't see them. But in Inuvik and other Arctic towns where the land is permanently frozen, the only place to put the pipes is above the ground. At first, it seemed strange to see those pipes everywhere, but after a while I stopped noticing them. It was harder to ignore the people out on the streets — the bright colours of some of their parkas, mitts, and hats really stood out against the snow.

We had come here to sell Bill's goods, so we didn't waste any time getting to work.

**See the ferry to the left? During summer, it carries vehicles across the Mackenzie River.**

**It's hard to miss the Igloo Church in Inuvik. Bill set up shop in his trailer near the "igloo."**

First we parked the trailer downtown, in a lot near the Igloo Church. Then we drove the tractor to the house Bill owned in Inuvik. He kept a van at his house and we jumped in it to deliver some supplies. Finally, we returned to the trailer. We were ready to transform it into a store.

We carried some steel stairs up to the side opening of the trailer and added a door, like the kind on a house, to the opening. Inside, Bill marked prices on a blackboard, while I clipped some display shelves on the walls. We both carried out the produce boxes, opened them, then waited for the first customers to arrive.

While we waited, I walked through the "store" and looked again at the goods we had brought with us from the south. There were watermelons, two kinds of cabbages, five kinds of apples, and oranges, lemons, limes, and tangerines. I moved a carton of kiwi fruit next to the grapes, then checked out the peppers (yellow, red, green, and hot ones), bok choy and bean sprouts,

When customers walk up to Bill's "store" in Inuvik, this is what they usually see (main photo). At some stops, shoppers see the cab at the front too (above).

Like anyone who runs a store that sells groceries and produce, Bill uses a scale for weighing many of his goods (above). The prices he charges are marked on a big board for everyone to see (right).

tomatoes and cucumbers. We even had wildflower blossoms for sale. Some people liked to eat them in a salad. And that didn't include everything else that was for sale. Bill had brought back bacon and dog food, soap and cereal, and more …

Many people in Inuvik like Bill's fruits and vegetables better than the produce in the local stores because Bill's produce is fresher. The local stores order their produce by phone from a warehouse in the south, like the ones we shopped at, and have to take whatever the warehouse sends them, even if the lettuce is wilted and the apples are badly bruised.

"I didn't think much of Bill's produce when I first saw it," one customer told me with a smile as we stood by the vegetables. "I thought cauliflower was supposed to have black spots on it — but it's not!"

I helped him carry some groceries, including an entire carton of cauliflower, outside to his toboggan. After I said good-bye, I watched him drag his groceries down the street. Then I stepped back in the store to help other shoppers load their purchases on their toboggans and in their cars. In snow-covered Inuvik, toboggans as well as cars were some of the "vehicles" people had for hauling their groceries home from Bill's store!

After the last load of groceries had left, it was finally time to close up shop and turn the store back into a truck. "We've got a big day coming up tomorrow," grinned Bill as he swept the floor and I stacked some cartons. "And I don't just mean selling groceries up in Tuktoyaktuk. Getting to Tuk is the real adventure. Let's hope there aren't any high winds — one good whiteout and we could end up lost!"

As we left Inuvik and drove onto the river,
I felt anxious and excited. I had always
wanted to spend time travelling on an ice
road – and now I was about to do just that!

# Chapter 8

# Strange, Dangerous Ice

As Bill drove our truck onto the Mackenzie River, I thought about the ice road we were on. Under the ice flowed dangerous waters, deep enough to drown in, if the shocking cold didn't kill you first. I glanced out the window at the ice road and shivered …

There appeared to be enough ice if you wanted to pull on some skates and skim safely over the frozen river. But was there enough ice to support Bill's tractor and trailer loaded with groceries? I found the answer on the signs by the sides of the road. According to them, the ice was thick enough for big rigs to drive on. Still, I thought about the icy water. I

Beaufort Sea

Tuktoyaktuk

Mackenzie River

Inuvik ⊕

This was the end of the ice road and the last stop on our trip to the far north. What would we find in Tuk? I wondered ...

When we drove onto the ice road, it felt like we were on a very bumpy ice rink. Everything around us — the road, the snow-banks, the land — was white and looked the same to me.

We left the river road behind and drove onto the sea. The ice was black and looked as smooth as glass.

An ice road is a two-way street. As we drove north, we passed some other cars heading south.

**Everything from lumber to lemons travels by truck on the ice roads. It's easy to forget that this road is made of frozen water — until you spot the ice beneath the snow.**

reminded myself that we had driven over river ice yesterday without any problems. But driving across a river, from one side to the other, and driving along a river are two different things. Yesterday, we had been on two ice roads for about ten minutes each time. Today, we would spend part of an entire day — not minutes, but hours and hours — driving on the Mackenzie River all the way to the Beaufort Sea. For the final part of our trip, we would actually leave the river ice road and drive on another kind of ice road, one that ran over the solid ice of the Beaufort Sea.

I felt anxious … and very excited. I had always wanted to see the ice roads of the far north and today was the day I would really experience them for myself!

"An ice road that runs over a lake is smoother to drive on than a river road, like this one," Bill told me, as we slowly bumped our way along the river.

"But lake roads aren't perfect. I have heard many stories about people who have crashed through the ice on a lake. Only the lucky ones survive.

"Fred Oberg … now he was one of the lucky ones. He worked on Lake Athabasca, way east of here in northern Saskatchewan. Fred's job was to prepare an ice road on the lake. To do that, he had to drive a grader, a heavy machine used on roads, over the snow-covered ice. Fred had a dangerous job — as I told you yesterday, the snow holds in the heat, leaving soft spots in the ice that you can't see until it's too late.

"Fred was out on the ice when it suddenly broke under him. If Fred had been driving a truck, he would have had more warning when the ice cracked — trucks

# Making Tracks in the North

**With skis at the front and wheels that run inside sturdy belts, a snowmobile can go places that a truck can't: off roads, over deep snow, and into the bush. Snowmobile travel is lots of fun, but for comfort and warmth nothing beats a big truck!**

usually float for a few seconds before they go down and that gives you time to open the door and jump out of the truck. But Fred was driving a grader and the grader sank straight to the bottom of the lake, taking Fred all the way with it."

"So how was Fred lucky?" I asked. "It doesn't sound very lucky to end up on the bottom of a lake in the middle of winter!"

"Maybe not," agreed Bill with a grin. "But here's where Fred did get lucky. First of all, he had to get out of the grader, swim up to the ice, and find the hole that he had crashed through. He found the hole — that was his first piece of luck. His second bit of luck came after he climbed onto the ice and headed for the shore and help. He was soaking wet and the cold might have killed him if a truck hadn't passed by, picked him up, and brought him to a camp down the road. Fred survived, but he didn't drive a grader on the lake again."

After hearing all the story, I had to agree with Bill: Fred did seem to be one

# More Ways to Make Tracks

**Planes are used year-round to carry goods to the Arctic, but flying in goods is more expensive than hauling them by truck over the ice roads. Small aircraft, like the two planes in this photo, can use open spaces as runways during takeoffs and landings.**

lucky and tough guy. He could have ended up like another driver I had heard about named Larry Grier. Larry drove a heavy tractor on the same ice road as Fred Oberg and Larry was about as unlucky as you can get. When Larry was out on the lake, a piece of ice broke under him and tipped, dumping Larry and his tractor into the water. Then the ice tipped back, sealing the hole shut. Unlike Fred, Larry didn't have a chance to reach the hole and climb out. His body was never recovered.

With stories like the one about Larry, it was easy to wonder what Bill and I were doing on an ice road in the first place. We weren't the only ones around — I noticed another truck far ahead of us and we had passed some cars going the other way. Lots of people used the ice roads. Why didn't everybody simply find another way to get around in the north?

The answer was simple: there is no other way to reach parts of the far north by land. Take the route we were on. This ice

Estelle Pielak

# Kidding Around in the Arctic

Isaac Lennie

**W**hat do kids love about living in the Arctic? When some kids from Inuvik were asked that question, they came up with these cool answers.

In January, we have fireworks at the "Sunrise Festival". That's where we celebrate the return of the sun after a month of darkness.

Sarah MacNabb

I like to watch the northern lights.

Faye Apsimik

I've lived in Inuvik all my life. I like it here in the winter because you can go snowmobiling and snowboarding. Every spring, we have a "Muskrat Jamboree" with snowmobile, snowshoe, and toboggan pull races.

Samuel Anderson

During the summer, when there is 24 hours of light each day, we have picnics and play outside at night. We also have drum dancing in Inuvik. I like "Midnight Madness", when we celebrate the longest day of the year in June.

Crystal Lee Saunders

There's lots of great things to do here. There are whaling camps, summer day camps, a library, and a youth centre where you can play video games. We have a holiday called the "Sunrise Festival" that has fireworks. That's my favourite holiday.

Jessica Davis

In the winter I like snowmobiling and playing in the snow. In the summer there is no snow at all and we get 24 hours of daylight, so we can play outside any time.
Megan Nussbaumer

In summer, we have 24 hours of daylight and I can go biking, skateboarding, and rollerblading. In winter, I like to watch hockey at the arena and go snowmobiling.
Vaughn Gordon

I like Inuvik because there are a lot of different people here. There are Inuit, French, Chinese, Dene, Japanese, Filipino, Arabic, English and more.
Chad Hunt

We celebrate the "Muskrat Jamboree" and the "Sunrise Festival." There are special activities for kids at the celebrations, like kids' carnivals. There is always something to do here!
Graeme Reid

road is the only land route to Tuktoyaktuk and it's only open for several months during the long winter. During spring, summer, and fall, when the ice isn't around, there's only water, swamp, and permafrost left. It's impossible to build a regular road on water and next to impossible to build one on swamp and permanently frozen ground.

So why don't people forget the land routes completely and travel by air instead? Airplanes are used year-round to carry people and cargo from the south to the north and back.

However, flying in groceries, produce, and fuel is more expensive than hauling them by truck over the ice roads. Ice roads make it possible for people in the far north to get goods they couldn't otherwise afford to purchase.

An ice road is a two-way street: it's the way many goods reach the north and it's also the way people in the far north get out of town. Northerners use ice roads to reach other communities by car, van, and pickup truck, something they can't do for most of the year. As dangerous as they are at times, ice roads provide important lifelines to other places, people, and goods.

A loud "p-p-p-p-pop!" just outside my window interrupted my thoughts. I peered down at the ice. Up to now, it had looked white and bumpy. But now, I noticed, the ice was black. It looked as smooth as glass, like the lake ice Bill had been telling me about.

"That black ice is sea ice," said Bill, when I pointed it out to him. "We're on the Beaufort Sea now. It won't be long before we reach the end of the ice road. Our next stop is Tuktoyaktuk!"

When warm weather comes and the ice road melts away, the only way to reach Tuktoyaktuk from the south is by plane. The view over Tuk is great — but flying here isn't half the Arctic adventure that driving on the ice road is!

# Chapter 9

# Back on Solid Ground

We left the smooth sea ice behind and we rolled over Kugmallit Bay toward the harbour. It was noon and still dark out – almost as dark as when we had left Inuvik – but I could easily make out ships locked in the ice and some buildings beyond them. We

had done it. We had travelled over the ice roads all the way to Tuktoyaktuk!

"I've always wanted to know what Tuk is like in the spring or summer," Bill said, as TD jumped into his lap and looked over the steering wheel. "The only time I ever get to see it is in the

# Where Am I Now?

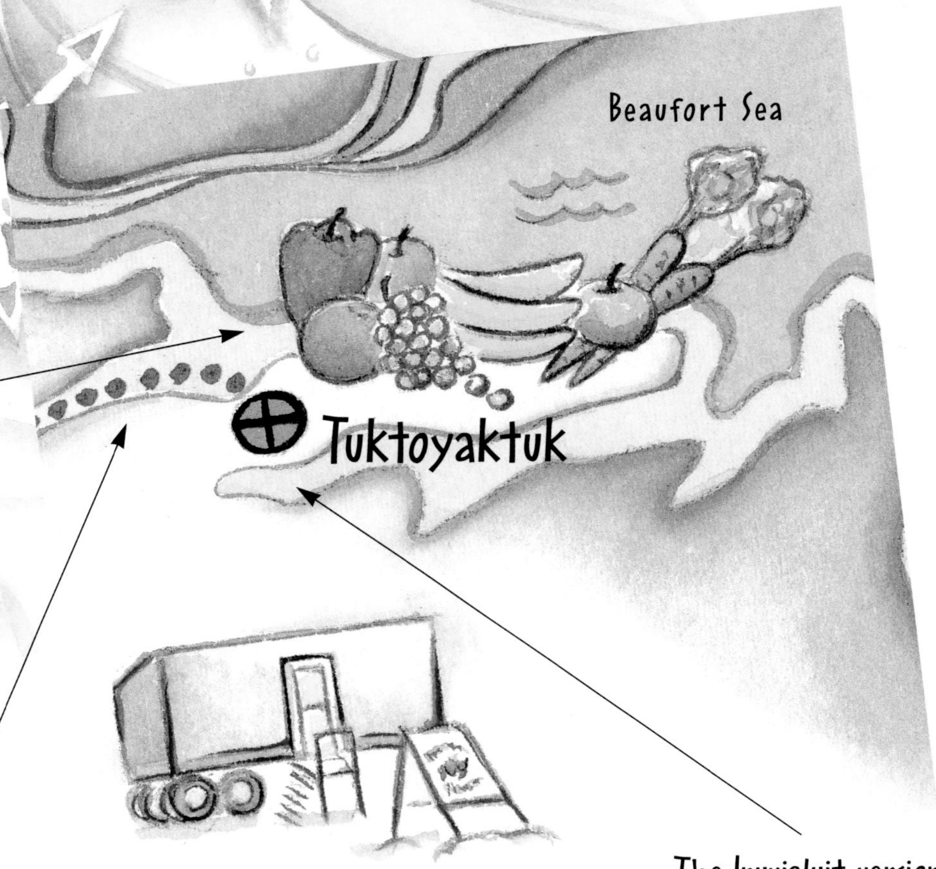

Beaufort Sea

⊕ Tuktoyaktuk

In the summer, you can see beluga whales in the water here. There is also a reindeer grazing area nearby, on the land.

It took less than a day to drive from Inuvik to Tuk. During that time, I came away with enough memories to last a lifetime.

The Inuvialuit version of Tuktoyaktuk means "looks like a caribou." Some people think that, during low tide, the reefs of Tuk resemble these moose relatives.

**As we wheeled our way across the bay to the tiny town of Tuk, I spotted these ships in the ice.**

middle of winter when I bring my rig here. But maybe I'm not missing much – Tuk's not exactly what you'd call a big city."

Bill was right: Tuktoyaktuk is a tiny town, even smaller than Inuvik. Long ago, it had been the place where whale-hunting native people called the Inuvialuit lived. These days it's known as a base for people who are involved in the oil and gas exploration that sometimes happens in this part of the Arctic. I looked around at the houses sprinkled over the snow-covered, gravelly land by the sea and I wondered what it would be like to live and work here.

Suddenly, I understood – really understood – why the ice road was important to the people of Tuk. For me, the ice road had been a route to take for some adventure

and fun. But for the people who live here, the ice road is essential. It's their link to the rest of the world and all the good things that come from other places. The people of Tuk would really appreciate Bill's fresh produce from the south – I looked forward to seeing the delighted expressions on their faces as they held fresh heads of lettuce and juicy oranges in their hands!

Much later, after we had sold the last of Bill's goods, I was still thinking about the pleased looks that were on the faces of his customers. As I cleaned up, Bill handed me my parka and mitts. "Come on," he said. "There's something outside you won't want to miss, but you have to hurry."

We stepped onto the snow and gazed up at a wavy panel of northern lights. It

# Pop Goes the Pingo!

**T**ake a trip around Tuktoyaktuk and you'll find that much of the land here is flat, except for unusual hills popping up in many places. These hills, which look like little volcanos, are called pingos and they're only found in parts of the Arctic. Pingos are created by underground water that freezes, pushing the ground upward. "Baby" pingos can grow up to .5 metres (20 inches) in a single year. By the time they are "adults" some pingos may be the height of a small apartment building or taller. One of the best-known pingos in Tuktoyaktuk, named "Ibyuk," is about 50 metres (165 feet) high. Scientists estimate that Ibyuk has been around for roughly a thousand years — that means it was about 300 years old when Marco Polo made his legendary trip from Europe to China!

# And the Beat Goes On ...

**Inuit people, called the Inuvialuit, who live in this part of the Arctic have traditions which still exist today. One of those traditions is drum dancing (see above). The dancers sing and act out stories about animals, hunts, and past events. In some communities, elders teach kids how to drum dance so that one day the kids will be able to pass on drum dancing to their kids and help keep this tradition alive.**

looked like a gigantic line of tie-dyed sheets hung out to dry in the wind. When I turned to Bill, puzzled, he put a finger to his lips, then cupped his hands over his ears. I listened carefully – and that's when I heard a soft hissing and crackling sound. The noise was coming from the "sheets!"

Together, we stood silently listening to the mysterious sound. After a while, TD stopped barking and stood next to us with her head cocked toward the lights. She looked like she was listening to them, too.

There are some people who would say that what we were hearing wasn't the northern lights: it was just our overactive imaginations. But I like to believe what some native people believe — that the northern lights are also "talking lights." I didn't know what made the sounds in the sky and I didn't really care. All that mattered to me at this moment was enjoying every last hiss and crackle.

The sounds finally faded away and I thought about Marco Polo and the other ancient merchant adventurers. Like them, we had travelled to distant places, had seen many strange sights, and we carried with us memories of all that we had experienced along the way.

As I followed Bill back to the trailer, I recalled the other unexpected things I had seen on our journey to this place … the wolf with its tail floating behind it … the tiny, ancient trees that might grow forever … the mysterious island that ended up in the river … the first time I had seen the northern lights and felt as small and unimportant as a snowflake.

And then there were the ice roads. Now that I had spent hours driving on one, I understood why some people just couldn't get enough of the ice roads. I was eager to climb back in the truck and drive on the Mackenzie River one more time.

I took one last look at the lights and smiled. Our northern journey was over, but there was still the long drive home, beginning early tomorrow.

Who could tell what we might find?

# INDEX

airplanes, 75, 77
apples, 10, 12
Arctic Circle, 52, 54, 55, 57, 65

Barkerville, 26, 28
Beaufort Sea, 73, 77
beluga whales, 80
Burns Lake, 36

camels, 27, 32-33
caribou, 54, 56, 80
Cariboo gold rush, 25
CB radio (citizen band radio), 39
Chilkoot Pass, 43
children in Inuvik, 76-77
Coco, 20
cold weather, 29, 45-46, 52, 53

Dawson City, 42-43, 45-47, 49
daylight hours above the Arctic
    Circle, 65
Dease Lake, 40
Dempster, Corporal, 49
Dempster Highway, 44, 46, 49
Dene Indians, 77
dogsleds, 58-59
drum dancing, 83

Eagle Plains, 53-54

falling rocks, 26, 27, 29, 36, 39
ferries, 65
Fort McPherson, 49
Fraser River, 24
Fraser River gold rush, 25, 27
frostbite, 48

gold rush, 25, 27-28, 42, 47

hoarfrost, 45-46

Ibyuk (pingo), 82
ice roads, 8, 37, 62, 63, 70-71, 72, 77
    accidents on, 73-75
    lake roads and river roads, 73-75
Inuit people, 55. See also Inuvialuit
Inuvialuit
    drum dancing, 83
    meaning of "Tuktoyaktuk," 80
Inuvik, 6, 62, 64, 69
    activities in, 76-77
    cultural mix in, 77
    Igloo Church, 62, 66

jade, 36, 38-40

Kitwanga, 36, 37
Klondike gold rush, 42-43, 44, 47

logs, 13-14
"Lost Patrol," 44, 46, 48-49

Mackenzie River, 63, 65, 71
maps, 2-3, 10, 18, 26, 36, 44, 52, 62,
    72, 80
Marco Polo, 6
"Midnight Madness," 76
moose, 5, 35, 36, 40, 41
"Muskrat Jamboree," 77

northern lights, 50-51, 52, 55, 81,
    83-84
Northwest Territories, 2
Nunavut, 2

Peel River, 63
pingos, 82

pipes, 64

reindeer grazing area, 80
Royal Canadian Mounted Police, 59
Royal Northwest Mounted Police,
    44, 49
Rutherford, Bill, 6, 36
    Bill's truck-store, 6, 10, 13, 64,
    66-69, 81

Skagway, 44
snowmobiles, 59
sounds
    ice roads, 62, 63
    northern lights, 55, 83-84
"Sunrise Festival," 76-77

TD, The Dog, 10, 11, 13, 17, 34
toboggans, 69
totem poles, 36, 37
Trans Canada Highway, 25
trees, 45-46, 52, 53
truck stops, 16-17, 19-20, 22-23
Trucker Buddy International Inc., 21
truckers, 19
trucks, 10, 15, 36-37, 46, 48
    accommodation inside, 26, 29-31,
    33, 44
Tuktoyaktuk, 6, 78-79, 80, 82

utilidors, 62, 64

Vancouver, 6

wind, 14-15
    at Eagle Plains, 53-4
wolves, 26, 33, 40, 60-61, 62, 63

## FURTHER RESOURCES: WEBSITES

Timber Wolf Information Network at:          **http://www.timberwolfinformation.org/**
    *This website includes a multimedia gallery with attention-grabbing photos and audio files, a "kids only"*
*section, and lots of links to other wolf sites.*

Auroras: Paintings in the Sky at:          **http://www.exploratorium.edu/learning_studio/auroras/**
    *Here's a self-guided tour that answers all your questions about the northern lights and even shows you*
*what they look like from space.*

Inuvik Home Page at:          **http://ruis.pair.com/inuviktv/inuviknet/**
    *To get a taste of life in the Inuvik region, visit this website. You can browse through a photo diary of Inuvik,*
*catch up on community events, and explore many other links filled with current information about the far north.*

Government of the Northwest Territories (GNWT) Home Page at:          **http://www.gov.nt.ca/**
    *Amazing facts about the far north, a special section for kids, and information about the territory of*
*Nunavut are just some of the things you'll find on this easy-to-use website.*

# ACKNOWLEDGEMENTS

Thanks to Bill Rutherford, a modern merchant-adventurer who showed me that the spirit of Marco Polo lives in the Canadian north.

—Andy Turnbull

Many thanks to Andy Turnbull, who introduced me to the subject of ice roads and answered my many truck and travel questions, and to Rick Wilks of Annick Press, who invited me on the exciting adventure of creating this book, provided roadside assistance whenever I needed it, and allowed me time to savour the sights along the way. Special thanks and much appreciation go out to Sheryl Shapiro for the expertise and care she lavished on the design of this attractive book and for being such a pleasure to work with, no matter how late the hour or how pressing the deadline. Thanks to Tina Forrester for diligently and cheerfully tracking down photographs and research materials and for generally assisting with the fact-checking of the final text. As well, thanks go out to Chum McLeod for her wonderful map, and to Mary Ellen Binder and her class at Sir Alexander Mackenzie School in Inuvik, who shared their thoughts about life in the far north and supplied other information as requested. And lastly, my work on this book would not have been possible without my husband, Michael, who answered my scientific and technical questions, encouraged me when the going got tough, and was always there to welcome me home after a hard day of writing about life on the road.

—Debora Pearson

Many thanks to the people and organizations who generously contributed photographs and information. The pictures they supplied appear on the following pages: British Columbia Archives, 27, 32, 37; Canadian Parks Service, 41, Dart Transit Company, 19, 20; Dawson City Museum and Historical Society, 42–43, 46, 48–49; Inuvialuit Regional Corporation, 74, 82; Jedway Enterprises, Watson Lake, Yukon, 38; John Mitchell, Earth Images Foundation, 63; Lynn and Donna Rogers, 60; MacMillan Bloedel Limited, 14; Mitchie Creek Mushing, 58, Whitehorse; Navistar International Corporation Canada, 30 (top), 31 (below); Sir Alexander Mackenzie School, Inuvik, 76–77; Sterling Truck Corporation, 30 (bottom), 31 (inset); Tessa Macintosh Photography, 50–51, 83, 84–85; TGIT Geomatics, 78–79; Tourism and Parks, Northwest Territories, Inuvik Region, 46, 54, 55; Tourism British Columbia, 12, 28; Trucker Buddy International Inc., 21. All other photographs by Andy Turnbull. Many thanks also to Western Arctic District for the information they supplied.

Special thanks to Stephen Gundale at Dart Transit Company and to Mary Ellen Binder of Sir Alexander Mackenzie School in Inuvik, both of whom went way further than the proverbial extra mile.

—Tina Forrester

**In the same series:**
*52 Days by Camel: My Sahara Adventure*
**by Lawrie Raskin with Debora Pearson**

To the truckers and traders of the world, who have been important to every civilization in human history and who make the world we know possible.

—A.T.

For my son, Benjamin, a small boy with a huge love of trucks.

—D.P.

We acknowledge the support of the Canada Council for the Arts for our publishing program. We also thank the Ontario Arts Council.

THE CANADA COUNCIL | LE CONSEIL DES ARTS
FOR THE ARTS | DU CANADA
SINCE 1957 | DEPUIS 1957

**Cataloguing in Publication Data**

Turnbull, Andy
By truck to the north : my Arctic adventure

Includes index.
ISBN 1-55037-551-2 (bound)  ISBN 1-55037-550-4 (pbk.)

1. British Columbia – Juvenile literature. 2. Canada, Northern – Juvenile literature.
3. British Columbia – Description and travel – Juvenile literature. 4. Canada, Northern – Description and travel –
Juvenile literature. 5. Turnbull, Andy – Journeys – British Columbia – Juvenile literature.
6. Turnbull, Andy – Journeys – Canadian, Northern – Juvenile literature.
I. Pearson, Debora.  II. Title.

FC2956.T87 1998  1999    j971.9    C98-931599-1        F1060.35.T87 1998

The text was typeset in Apollo and AG Old Face.

Distributed in Canada by:
Firefly Books Ltd.
3680 Victoria Park Avenue
Willowdale, ON
M2H 3K1

Published in the U.S.A. by Annick Press (U.S.) Ltd.
Distributed in the U.S.A. by:
Firefly Books (U.S.) Inc.
P.O. Box 1338
Ellicott Station
Buffalo, NY 14205

Printed and bound in Canada by
Interglobe Printers Inc., Québec.